ETHICAL AND PROFESSIONAL STANDARDS

I   **Professionalism**
I (A)   Knowledge of the Law
I (B)   Independence and Objectivity
I (C)   Misrepresentation
I (D)   Misconduct
II   **Integrity of Capital Markets**
II (A)   Material Nonpublic Information
II (B)   Market Manipulation
III   **Duties to Clients**
III (A)   Loyalty, Prudence, and Care
III (B)   Fair Dealing
III (C)   Suitability
III (D)   Performance Presentation
III (E)   Preservation of Confidentiality
IV   **Duties to Employers**
IV (A)   Loyalty
IV (B)   Additional Compensation Arrangements
IV (C)   Responsibilities of Supervisors
V   **Investment Analysis, Recommendations, and Action**
V (A)   Diligence and Reasonable Basis
V (B)   Communication with Clients and Prospective Clients
V (C)   Record Retention
VI   **Conflicts of Interest**
VI (A)   Disclosure of Conflicts
VI (B)   Priority of Transactions
VI (C)   Referral Fees
VII   **Responsibilities as a CFA Institute Member or CFA Candidate**
VII (A)   Conduct in the CFA Program
VII (B)   Reference to CFA Institute, CFA Designation, and CFA Program

QUANTITATIVE METHODS

Simple Linear Regression
Correlation:
$$r_{XY} = \frac{cov_{XY}}{(s_X)(s_Y)}$$

t-test for r (n – 2 **df**): $t = \dfrac{r\sqrt{n-2}}{\sqrt{1-r^2}}$

Estimated slope coefficient: $\dfrac{cov_{xy}}{\sigma_x^2}$

Estimated intercept: $\hat{b}_0 = \bar{Y} - \hat{b}_1\bar{X}$

Confidence interval for predicted Y-value:
$$\hat{Y} \pm t_c \times SE \text{ of forecast}$$

Multiple Regression
$$Y_i = b_0 + (b_1 \times X_{1i}) + (b_2 \times X_{2i}) + (b_3 \times X_{3i}) + \varepsilon_i$$

- Test statistical significance of b; H_0: b = 0.

  $t = \hat{b} / s_{\hat{b}}$, n — k − 1 df

- Reject if |t| > critical t or p-value < α.

- Confidence Interval: $\hat{b}_j \pm \left(t_c \times s_{\hat{b}_j}\right)$.

- SST = RSS + SSE.
- MSR = RSS / k.
- MSE = SSE / (n − k − 1).

- Test statistical significance of regression:
  F = MSR / MSE with k and n − k − 1 df (1-tail).

- Standard error of estimate (SEE = $\sqrt{MSE}$). Smaller SEE means better fit.
- Coefficient of determination (R^2 = RSS / SST). % of variability of Y explained by Xs; higher R^2 means better fit.

Regression Analysis—Problems

- Heteroskedasticity. Non-constant error variance. Detect with Breusch-Pagan test. Correct with White-corrected standard errors.

- Autocorrelation. Correlation among error terms. Detect with Durbin-Watson test; positive autocorrelation if DW < d_l. Correct by adjusting standard errors using Hansen method.

- Multicollinearity. High correlation among Xs. Detect if F-test significant, t-tests insignificant. Correct by dropping X variables.

Model Misspecification

- Omitting a variable.
- Variable should be transformed.
- Incorrectly pooling data.
- Using lagged dependent vbl. as independent vbl.
- Forecasting the past.
- Measuring independent variables with error.

Effects of Misspecification
Regression coefficients are biased and inconsistent, lack of confidence in hypothesis tests of the coefficients or in the model predictions.

Linear trend model: $y_t = b_0 + b_1t + \varepsilon_t$

Log-linear trend model: $\ln(y_t) = b_0 + b_1t + \varepsilon_t$

Covariance stationary: mean and variance don't change over time. To determine if a time series is covariance stationary, (1) plot data, (2) run an AR model and test correlations, and/or (3) perform Dickey Fuller test.

Unit root: coefficient on lagged dep. vbl. = 1. Series with unit root is not covariance stationary. First differencing will often eliminate the unit root.
Autoregressive (AR) model: specified correctly if autocorrelation of residuals not significant.
Mean reverting level for AR(1):
$$\frac{b_0}{(1 - b_1)}$$

RMSE: square root of average squared error.
Random Walk Time Series:
$$x_t = x_{t-1} + \varepsilon_t$$

Seasonality: indicated by statistically significant lagged err. term. Correct by adding lagged term.
ARCH: detected by estimating:
$$\hat{\varepsilon}_t^2 = a_0 + a_1\hat{\varepsilon}_{t-1}^2 + \mu_t$$

Variance of ARCH series:
$$\hat{\sigma}_{t+1}^2 = \hat{a}_0 + \hat{a}_1\hat{\varepsilon}_t^2$$

Risk Types:

Appropriate method	Distribution of risk	Sequential?	Accommodates Correlated Variables?
Simulations	Continuous	Does not matter	Yes
Scenario analysis	Discrete	No	Yes
Decision trees	Discrete	Yes	No

ECONOMICS

bid-ask spread = ask quote − bid quote
Cross rates with bid-ask spreads:
$$\left(\frac{A}{C}\right)_{bid} = \left(\frac{A}{B}\right)_{bid} \times \left(\frac{B}{C}\right)_{bid}$$
$$\left(\frac{A}{C}\right)_{offer} = \left(\frac{A}{B}\right)_{offer} \times \left(\frac{B}{C}\right)_{offer}$$

Currency arbitrage: "Up the bid and down the ask."
Forward premium = (forward price) − (spot price)
Value of fwd currency contract prior to expiration:
$$V_t = \frac{(FP_t - FP)(\text{contract size})}{\left[1 + R_A\left(\frac{days}{360}\right)\right]}$$

Covered interest rate parity:
$$F = \frac{\left[1 + R_A\left(\frac{days}{360}\right)\right]S_0}{\left[1 + R_B\left(\frac{days}{360}\right)\right]}$$

Uncovered interest rate parity:
$$E(\%\Delta S)_{(A/B)} = R_A - R_B$$

Fisher relation:
$$R_{nominal} = R_{real} + E(\text{inflation})$$

International Fisher Relation:
$$R_{nominal\,A} - R_{nominal\,B} = E(\text{inflation}_A) - E(\text{inflation}_B)$$

Relative Purchasing Power Parity: High inflation rates leads to currency depreciation.
$$\%\Delta S(A/B) = \text{inflation}_{(A)} - \text{inflation}_{(B)}$$
where: %ΔS(A/B) = change in spot price (A/B)
Profit on FX Carry Trade = interest differential − change in the spot rate of investment currency.
Mundell-Fleming model: Impact of monetary and fiscal policies on interest rates & exchange rates. Under high capital mobility, expansionary monetary policy/restrictive fiscal policy → low interest rates → currency depreciation. Under low capital mobility, expansionary monetary policy/ expansionary fiscal policy → current account deficits → currency depreciation.
Dornbusch overshooting model: Restrictive monetary policy → short-term appreciation of currency, then slow depreciation to PPP value.
Labor Productivity:
output per worker $Y/L = T(K/L)^\alpha$
Growth Accounting:
growth rate in potential GDP
= long-term growth rate of technology
+ α (long-term growth rate of capital)
+ (1 − α) (long-term growth rate of labor)
growth rate in potential GDP
= long-term growth rate of labor force
+ long-term growth rate in labor productivity

Classical Growth Theory
- Real GDP/person reverts to subsistence level.

Neoclassical Growth Theory
- Sustainable growth rate is a function of population growth, labor's share of income, and the rate of technological advancement.
- Growth rate in labor productivity driven only by improvement in technology.

continued on next page...

- Assumes diminishing returns to capital.

$$g^* = \frac{\theta}{(1-\alpha)} \qquad G^* = \frac{\theta}{(1-\alpha)} + \Delta L$$

Endogenous Growth Theory
- Investment in capital can have constant returns.
- ↑ in savings rate → permanent ↑ in growth rate.
- R&D expenditures ↑ technological progress.

Classifications of Regulations
- *Statutes:* Laws made by legislative bodies.
- *Administrative regulations:* Issued by government.
- *Judicial law:* Findings of the court.

Classifications of Regulators
- Can be government agencies or independent.
- Independent regulator can be SRO or non-SRO.

Self-Regulation in Financial Markets
- Independent SROs are more prevalent in common-law countries than in civil-law countries.

Economic Rationale for Regulatory Intervention
- *Informational frictions* arise in the presence of information asymmetry.
- *Externalities* deal with provision of public goods.

Regulatory Interdependencies and Their Effects
Regulatory capture theory: Regulatory body is influenced or controlled by industry being regulated.
Regulatory arbitrage: Exploiting regulatory differences between jurisdictions, or difference between substance and interpretation of a regulation.

Tools of Regulatory Intervention
- Price mechanisms, restricting or requiring certain activities, and provision of public goods or financing of private projects.

Regulations Covering Commerce
- Company law, tax law, contract law, competition law, banking law, bankruptcy law, and dispute resolution system.

Financial market regulations: Seek to protect investors and to ensure stability of financial system.
Securities market regulations: Include disclosure requirements, regulations to mitigate agency conflicts, and regulations to protect small investors.
Prudential supervision: Monitoring institutions to reduce system-wide risks and protect investors.

Anticompetitive Behaviors and Antitrust Laws
- Discriminatory pricing, bundling, exclusive dealing.
- Mergers leading to excessive market share blocked.

Net regulatory burden: Costs to the regulated entities minus the private benefits of regulation.
Sunset clauses: Require a cost-benefit analysis to be revisited before the regulation is renewed.

FINANCIAL STATEMENT ANALYSIS

Accounting for Intercorporate Investments
Investment in Financial Assets: <20% owned, no significant influence.
- Held-to-maturity at cost on balance sheet; interest and realized gain/loss on income statement.
- Available-for-sale at FMV with unrealized gains/losses in equity on B/S; dividends, interest, realized gains/losses on I/S.
- Held-for-trading at FMV; dividends, interest, realized and unrealized gains/losses on I/S.
- Designated as fair value – like held for trading.

Investments in Associates: 20–50% owned, significant influence. With equity method, pro-rata share of the investee's earnings incr. B/S inv. acct., also in I/S. Div. received decrease investment account (div. not in I/S).

Business Combinations: >50% owned, control. Acquisition method required under U.S. GAAP and IFRS. Goodwill not amortized, subject to annual impairment test. All assets, liabilities, revenue, and expenses of subsidiary are combined with parent, excluding intercomp. trans. If <100%, minority interest acct. for share not owned.

Joint Venture: 50% shared control. Equity method.

Financial Effect of Choice of Method
Equity, acquisition, & proportionate consolidation:
- All three methods report same net income.
- Assets, liabilities, equity, revenues, and expenses are higher under acquisition compared to the equity method.

Differences between IFRS and U.S. GAAP treatment of intercorporate investments include:
- Unrealized FX gains and losses on available-for-sale debt securities recognized on income statement under IFRS and as OCI under U.S. GAAP.
- IFRS permits either the "partial goodwill" or "full goodwill" methods to value goodwill and noncontrolling interest. U.S. GAAP requires the full goodwill method.

Pension Accounting
- PBO components: current service cost, interest cost, actuarial gains/losses, benefits paid.

Balance Sheet
- Funded status = plan assets – PBO = balance sheet asset (liability) under GAAP and IFRS.

Income Statement
- Total periodic pension cost (under both IFRS and GAAP) = contributions – Δ funded status.
- IFRS and GAAP differ on where the total periodic pension cost (TPPC) is reflected (Income statement vs. OCI).
- Under GAAP, periodic pension cost in P&L = service cost + interest cost ± amortization of actuarial (gains) and losses + amortization of past service cost – expected return on plan assets.
- Under IFRS, reported pension expense = service cost + past service cost + net interest expense.
- Under IFRS, discount rate = expected rate of return on plan assets. Net interest expense = discount rate × beginning funded status. If funded status was positive, a net interest income would be recognized.

Total Periodic Pension Cost
TPPC = ending PBO – beginning PBO + benefits paid – actual return on plan assets

TPPC = contributions – (ending funded status – beginning funded status)

Cash Flow Adjustment
If TPPC < firm contribution, difference = Δ in PBO (reclassify difference from CFF to CFO after-tax). If TPPC > firm contribution, diff = borrowing (reclassify difference from CFO to CFF after-tax).

Multinational Operations: Choice of Method
For self-contained sub, functional ≠ presentation currency; use current rate method:
- Assets/liabilities at current rate.
- Common stock at historical rate.
- Income statement at average rate.
- Exposure = shareholders' equity.
- Dividends at rate when paid.

For integrated sub., functional = presentation currency, use temporal method:
- Monetary assets/liabilities at current rate.
- Nonmonetary assets/liabilities at historical rate.
- Sales, SGA at average rate.
- COGS, depreciation at historical rate.
- Exposure = monetary assets – monetary liabilities.

Net asset position & depr. foreign currency = loss.
Net liab. position & depr. foreign currency = gain.

Original F/S vs. All-Current
- Pure BS and IS ratios unchanged.
- If LC depreciating (appreciating), translated mixed ratios will be larger (smaller).

Hyperinflation: GAAP vs. IFRS
Hyperinfl. = cumul. infl. > 100% over 3 yrs. GAAP: use temporal method. IFRS: 1st, restate foreign curr. st. for infl. 2nd, translate with current rates. Net purch. power gain/loss reported in income.

Beneish model: Used to detect earnings manipulation based on eight variables.

High-quality earnings are:
1. Sustainable: Expected to recur in future.
2. Adequate: Cover company's cost of capital.

IFRS AND U.S. GAAP DIFFERENCES

Reclassification of passive investments:
IFRS – Restricts reclassification into/out of FVPL.
U.S. GAAP – No such restriction.

Impairment losses on passive investments:
IFRS – Reversal allowed if due to specific event.
U.S. GAAP – No reversal of impairment losses.

Fair value accounting, investment in associates:
IFRS – Only for venture capital, mutual funds, etc.
U.S. GAAP – Fair value accounting allowed for all.

Goodwill impairment processes:
IFRS – 1 step (recoverable amount vs. carrying value)
U.S. GAAP – 2 steps (identify; measure amount)

Acquisition method contingent asset recognition:
IFRS – Contingent assets are not recognized.
U.S. GAAP – Recognized; recorded at fair value.

Prior service cost:
IFRS – Recognized as an expense in P&L.
U.S. GAAP – Reported in OCI; amortized to P&L.

Actuarial gains/losses:
IFRS – Remeasurements in OCI and not amortized.
U.S. GAAP – OCI, amortized with corridor approach.

Dividend/interest income and interest expense:
IFRS – Either operating or financing cash flows.
U.S. GAAP – Must classify as operating cash flow.

ROE decomposed (extended DuPont equation)

$$\text{ROE} = \underbrace{\frac{\text{NI}}{\text{EBT}}}_{\substack{\text{Tax}\\\text{Burden}}} \times \underbrace{\frac{\text{EBT}}{\text{EBIT}}}_{\substack{\text{Interest}\\\text{Burden}}} \times \underbrace{\frac{\text{EBIT}}{\text{revenue}}}_{\substack{\text{EBIT}\\\text{Margin}}} \times$$

$$\underbrace{\frac{\text{revenue}}{\text{average assets}}}_{\substack{\text{Total Asset}\\\text{Turnover}}} \times \underbrace{\frac{\text{average assets}}{\text{average equity}}}_{\substack{\text{Financial}\\\text{Leverage}}}$$

Accruals Ratio (balance sheet approach)

$$\text{accruals ratio}^{BS} = \frac{(\text{NOA}_{END} - \text{NOA}_{BEG})}{(\text{NOA}_{END} + \text{NOA}_{BEG})/2}$$

Accruals Ratio (cash flow statement approach)

$$\text{accruals ratio}^{CF} = \frac{(\text{NI} - \text{CFO} - \text{CFI})}{(\text{NOA}_{END} + \text{NOA}_{BEG})/2}$$

CORPORATE FINANCE

Capital Budgeting Expansion
- Initial outlay = FCInv + WCInv
- CF = $(S - C - D)(1 - T) + D = (S - C)(1 - T) + DT$
- TNOCF = $\text{Sal}_T + \text{NWCInv} - T(\text{Sal}_T - B_T)$

Capital Budgeting Replacement
- Same as expansion, except current after-tax salvage of old assets reduces initial outlay.
- Incremental depreciation is Δ in depreciation.

Evaluating Projects with Unequal Lives
- Least common multiple of lives method.
- Equivalent annual annuity (EAA) method: annuity w/ PV equal to PV of project cash flows.

continued on next page...

Effects of Inflation

- Discount nominal (real) cash flows at nominal (real) rate; unexpected changes in inflation affect project profitability; reduces the real tax savings from depreciation; decreases value of fixed payments to bondholders; affects costs and revenues differently.

Capital Rationing

- If positive NPV projects > available capital, choose the combination with the highest NPV.

Real Options

- Timing, abandonment, expansion, flexibility, fundamental options.

Economic and Accounting Income

- Econ income = AT CF + Δ in project's MV.
- Econ dep. based on Δ in investment's MV.
- Econ income is calculated before interest expense (cost of capital is reflected in discount rate).
- Accounting income = revenues – expenses.
- Acc. dep'n based on original investment cost.
- Interest (financing costs) deducted before calculating accounting income.

Valuation Models

- Economic profit = NOPAT – \$WACC
- Market Value Added = $\sum_{t=1}^{\infty} \dfrac{EP_t}{(1+WACC)^t}$
- Residual income: = NI – equity charge; discounted at required return on equity.
- Claims valuation separates CFs based on equity claims (discounted at cost of equity) and debt holders (discounted at cost of debt).

MM Prop I (No Taxes): capital structure irrelevant (no taxes, transaction, or bankruptcy costs).

$$V_L = V_U$$

MM Prop II (No Taxes): increased use of cheaper debt increases cost of equity, no change in WACC.

$$r_e = r_0 + \frac{D}{E}(r_0 - r_d)$$

MM Proposition I (With Taxes): tax shield adds value, value is maximized at 100% debt.

$$V_L = V_U + (t \times d)$$

MM Proposition II (With Taxes): tax shield adds value, WACC is minimized at 100% debt.

$$r_e = r_0 + \frac{D}{E}(r_0 - r_d)(1 - T_c)$$

Investor Preference Theories

- MM's dividend irrelevance theory: In a no-tax/no-fee world, dividend policy is irrelevant because investors can create a homemade dividend.
- Dividend preference theory says investors prefer the certainty of current cash to future capital gains.
- Tax aversion theory: Investors are tax averse to dividends; prefer companies buy back shares.

Effective Tax Rate on Dividends

Double taxation or *split rate* systems:
    eff. rate = corp. rate + (1 – corp. rate)(indiv. rate)
Imputation system: effective tax rate is the shareholder's individual tax rate.

Signaling Effects of Dividend Changes

Initiation: ambiguous signal.
Increase: positive signal.
Decrease: negative signal unless management sees many profitable investment opportunities.

Price change when stock goes ex-dividend:

$$\Delta P = \frac{D(1 - T_D)}{(1 - T_{CG})}$$

Target Payout Ratio Adjustment Model

If company earnings are expected to increase and the current payout ratio is below the target payout ratio, an investor can estimate future dividends through the following formula:

$$\text{expected dividend} = \binom{\text{previous}}{\text{dividend}} + \left[\binom{\text{expected}}{\substack{\text{increase} \\ \text{in EPS}}} \times \binom{\text{target}}{\substack{\text{payout} \\ \text{ratio}}} \times \binom{\text{adjustment}}{\text{factor}} \right]$$

Dividend Coverage Ratios

$$\text{dividend coverage ratio} = \text{net income} / \text{dividends}$$

FCFE coverage ratio
= FCFE / (dividends + share repurchases)

Share Repurchases

- Share repurchase is equivalent to cash dividend, assuming equal tax treatment.
- Unexpected share repurchase is good news.
- Rationale for: (1) potential tax advantages, (2) share price support/signaling, (3) added flexibility, (4) offsetting dilution from employee stock options, and (5) increasing financial leverage.

Dividend Policy Approaches

- Residual dividend: dividends based on earnings less funds retained to finance capital budget.
- Longer-term residual dividend: forecast capital budget, smooth dividend payout.
- Dividend stability: dividend growth aligned with sustainable growth rate.
- Target payout ratio: long-term payout ratio target.

Stakeholder impact analysis (SIA): Forces firm to identify the most critical groups.

Ethical Decision Making

Friedman Doctrine: Only responsibility is to increase profits "within the rules of the game."
Utilitarianism: Produce the highest good for the largest number of people.
Kantian ethics: People are more than just an economic input and deserve dignity and respect.
Rights theories: Even if an action is legal, it may violate fundamental rights and be unethical.
Justice theories: Focus on a just distribution of economic output (e.g., "veil of ignorance").

Corporate Governance Objectives

- Mitigate conflicts of interest between (1) managers and shareholders, and (2) directors and shareholders.
- Ensure assets used to benefit investors and stakeholders.

Merger Types: horizontal, vertical, conglomerate.
Merger Motivations: achieve synergies, more rapid growth, increased market power, gain access to unique capabilities, diversify, personal benefits for managers, tax benefits, unlock hidden value, achieving international goals, and bootstrapping earnings.
Pre-Offer Defense Mechanisms: poison pills and puts, reincorporate in a state w/ restrictive takeover laws, staggered board elections, restricted voting rights, supermajority voting, fair price amendments, and golden parachutes.
Post-Offer Defense Mechanisms: litigation, greenmail, share repurch, leveraged recap, the "crown jewel," "Pac-Man," and "just say no" defenses, and white knight/white squire.
The Herfindahl-Hirschman Index (HHI): market power = sum of squared market shares for all industry firms. In a moderately-concentrated industry (HHI 1,000 to 1,800), a merger is likely to be challenged if HHI increases 100 points (or increases 50 points for HHI >1,800).

$$HHI = \sum_{i=1}^{n}(MS_i \times 100)^2$$

Methods to Determine Target Value

DCF method: target proforma FCF discounted at adjusted WACC.
Comparable company analysis: target value from relative valuation metrics on similar firms + takeover premium.
Comparable transaction analysis: target value from takeover transaction; takeover premium included.

Merger Valuations

Combined firm:

$$V_{AT} = V_A + V_T + S - C$$

Takeover premium (to target):

$$\text{Gain}_T = TP = P_T - V_T$$

Synergies (to acquirer):

$$\text{Gain}_A = S - TP = S - (P_T - V_T)$$

Merger Risk & Reward

Cash offer: acquirer assumes risk & receives reward.
Stock offer: some of risks & rewards shift to target. If higher confidence in synergies; acquirer prefers cash & target prefers stock.
Forms of divestitures: equity carve-outs, spin-offs, split-offs, and liquidations.

EQUITY

Holding period return:

$$= r = \frac{P_1 - P_0 + CF_1}{P_0} = \frac{P_1 + CF_1}{P_0} - 1$$

Required return: Minimum expected return an investor requires given an asset's characteristics.
Internal rate of return (IRR): Equates discounted cash flows to the current price.
Equity risk premium:
    required return = risk-free rate + ($\beta \times$ ERP)
Gordon growth model equity risk premium:
    = 1-yr forecasted dividend yield on market index
    + consensus long-term earnings growth rate
    – long-term government bond yield
Ibbotson-Chen equity risk premium

$$[1+\hat{i}] \times [1+\widehat{rEg}] \times [1+\widehat{PEg}] - 1 + \hat{Y} - \widehat{RF}$$

Models of required equity return:
- *CAPM:* $r_j = RF + (\text{equity risk premium} \times \beta_j)$
- *Multifactor model:* required return = RF + (risk premium)$_1$ + ... + (risk premium)$_n$
- *Fama-French:* $r_j = RF + \beta_{mkt,j} \times (R_{mkt} - RF)$ $+ \beta_{SMB,j} \times (R_{small} - R_{big}) + \beta_{HML,j} \times (R_{HBM} - R_{LBM})$
- *Pastor-Stambaugh model:* Adds a liquidity factor to the Fama-French model.
- *Macroeconomic multifactor models:* Uses factors associated with economic variables.
- *Build-up method:* r = RF + equity risk premium + size premium + specific-company premium

Blume adjustment:
adjusted beta = (2/3 × raw beta) + (1/3 × 1.0)
WACC = weighted average cost of capital

$$= \frac{MV_{debt}}{MV_{debt+equity}} r_d (1-T) + \frac{MV_{equity}}{MV_{debt+equity}} r_e$$

Discount cash flows to *firm* at *WACC*, and cash flows to *equity* at the *required return on equity*.

Discounted Cash Flow (DCF) Methods

Use dividend discount models (DDM) when:
- Firm has dividend history.
- Dividend policy is related to earnings.
- Minority shareholder perspective.

Use free cash flow (FCF) models when:
- Firm lacks stable dividend policy.
- Dividend policy not related to earnings.

continued on next page...

Debt service coverage ratio:

$$DSCR = \frac{\text{first-year NOI}}{\text{debt service}}$$

Loan-to-value (LTV) ratio:

$$LTV = \frac{\text{loan amount}}{\text{appraisal value}}$$

$$\text{equity dividend rate} = \frac{\text{first year cash flow}}{\text{equity}}$$

Net asset value approach to REIT share valuation:

estimated cash NOI
÷ assumed cap rate
= estimated value of operating real estate
+ cash & accounts receivable
− debt and other liabilities
= net asset value
÷ shares outstanding
= NAV/share

Price-to-FFO approach to REIT share valuation:

funds from operations (FFO)
÷ shares outstanding
= FFO/share
× sector average P/FFO multiple
= NAV/share

Price-to-AFFO approach to REIT share valuation:

funds from operations (FFO)
− non-cash rents
− recurring maintenance-type capital expenditures
= AFFO
÷ shares outstanding
= AFFO/share
× property subsector average P/AFFO multiple
= NAV/share

Discounted cash flow REIT share valuation:

value of a REIT share
= PV(dividends for years 1 through n)
+ PV(terminal value at the end of year n)

Private Equity

Sources of value creation: reengineer firm, favorable debt financing; superior alignment of interests between management and PE ownership.
Valuation issues (VC firms relative to Buyouts): DCF not as common; equity, not debt, financing.
Key drivers of equity return:
Buyout: ↑ of multiple at exit, ↓ in debt.
VC: pre-money valuation, the investment, and subsequent equity dilution.
Components of performance (LBO): earnings growth, ↑ of multiple at exit, ↓ in debt.
Exit routes (in order of exit value, high to low): IPOs secondary mkt sales; MBO; liquidation.
Performance Measurement: gross IRR = return from portfolio companies. Net IRR = relevant for LP, net of fees & carried interest.
Performance Statistics:
- PIC = % capital utilized by GP; cumulative sum of capital called down.
- Management fee: % of PIC.
- Carried interest: % carried interest × (change in NAV before distribution).
- NAV before distrib. = prior yr. NAV after distrib. + cap. called down − mgmt. fees + op. result.
- NAV after distributions = NAV before distributions − carried interest − distributions
- DPI multiple = (cumulative distributions) / PIC = LP's realized return.
- RVPI multiple = (NAV after distributions) / PIC = LP's unrealized return.
- TVPI mult. = DPI mult. + RVPI mult.

NPV VC & IRR methods: calculate pre-money value, post-money value, ownership fraction, & price per share. NPV methods starts with POST, IRR with expected future wealth.
Assessing Risk: (1) adjust discount rate for prob of failure; (2) use scenario analysis for term.

Commodities

Contango: futures prices > spot prices
Backwardation: futures prices < spot prices

Term Structure of Commodity Futures

1. **Insurance theory:** Contract buyers compensated for providing protection to commodity producers. Implies backwardation is normal.
2. **Hedging pressure hypothesis:** Like insurance theory, but includes both long hedgers (→ contango) and short hedgers (→ backwardation).
3. **Theory of storage:** Spot and futures prices related through storage costs and convenience yield.

Total return on fully collateralized long futures
= collateral return + price return + roll return
Roll return: positive in backwardation because long-dated contracts are cheaper than expiring contracts.

PORTFOLIO MANAGEMENT

Portfolio Management Planning Process

- Analyze risk and return objectives.
- Analyze constraints: liquidity, time horizon, legal and regulatory, taxes, unique circumstances.
- Develop IPS: client description, purpose, duties, objectives and constraints, performance review schedule, modification policy, rebalancing guidelines.

Arbitrage Pricing Theory

$$E(R_p) = R_F + \beta_{P,1}(\lambda_1) + \beta_{P,2}(\lambda_2) + \ldots + \beta_{P,k}(\lambda_k)$$

Expected return = risk free rate
+ Σ(factor sensitivity) × (factor risk premium)

Value at risk (VaR) is an estimate of the minimum loss that will occur with a given probability over a specified period, expressed as a currency amount or as percentage of portfolio value.

5% annual \$VaR = (Mean annual return − 1.65 × annual standard deviation) × portfolio value

Conditional VaR (CVaR) is the expected loss given that the loss exceeds the VaR.
Incremental VaR (IVaR) is the estimated change in VaR from a specific change in the size of a portfolio position.
Marginal VaR (MVaR) is the estimate of the change in VaR for a small change in a portfolio position and is used as an estimate of the position's contribution to overall VaR.

Variance for W_A% fund A + W_B% fund B

$$\sigma^2_{\text{Portfolio}} = W_A^2\sigma_A^2 + W_B^2\sigma_B^2 + 2W_A W_B Cov_{AB}$$

Annualized standard deviation
= $\sqrt{250}$ × (daily standard deviation)

% change in value vs. change in YTM
= −duration (ΔY) + ½ convexity (ΔY)²
for Macaulay duration, replace ΔY by ΔY/(1+Y)

Inter-temporal rate of substitution $= m_t = \dfrac{u_t}{u_0}$

$$= \frac{\text{marginal utility of consuming 1 unit in the future}}{\text{marginal utility of current consumption of 1 unit}}$$

Real risk-free rate of return $= \dfrac{1 - P_0}{P_0} = \left[\dfrac{1}{E(m_t)}\right] - 1$

Default-free, inflation indexed, zero coupon:

$$\text{Bond price} = P_0 = \frac{E(P_1)}{(1+R)} + cov(P_1, m_1)$$

Nominal short term interest rate (r)
= real risk-free rate (R) + expected inflation (π)

Nominal long term interest rate = R + π + θ
where θ = risk premium for inflation uncertainty

Break-even inflation rate (BEI)
= yield$_{\text{non-inflation indexed bond}}$ − yield$_{\text{inflation indexed bond}}$

BEI for longer maturity bonds
= expected inflation (π) + infl. risk premium (θ)

Credit risky bonds required return = R + π + θ + γ
where γ = risk premium (spread) for credit risk

Discount rate for equity = R + π + θ + γ + κ
λ = *equity risk premium* = γ + κ
γ = *risk premium for equity vs. risky debt*

Discount rate for commercial real estate
= R + π + θ + γ + κ + φ
κ = *terminal value risk*, φ = *illiquidity premium*

Multifactor model return attribution:

$$\text{factor return} = \sum_{i=1}^{k}(\beta_{pi} - \beta_{bi}) \times (\lambda_i)$$

Active return
= factor return + security selection return

Active risk squared
= active factor risk + active specific risk

Active specific risk $= \displaystyle\sum_{i=1}^{n}(w_{pi} - w_{bi})^2 \sigma_{\varepsilon i}^2$

Active return = portfolio return − benchmark return
$$R_A = R_P - R_B$$

Portfolio return $= R_P = \displaystyle\sum_{i=1}^{n} w_{P,i}R_i$

Benchmark return $= R_B = \displaystyle\sum_{i=1}^{n} w_{B,i}R_i$

Information ratio

$$= \frac{R_P - R_B}{\sigma_{(R_P - R_B)}} = \frac{R_A}{\sigma_A} = \frac{\text{active return}}{\text{active risk}}$$

Portfolio Sharpe ratio $= SR_P = \dfrac{R_P - R_F}{STD(R_P)}$

Optimal level of active risk:

Sharpe ratio $= \sqrt{SR_B^2 + IR_P^2}$

Total portfolio risk: $\sigma_P^2 = \sigma_B^2 + \sigma_A^2$

Information ratio: $IR = TC \times IC \times \sqrt{BR}$

Expected active return: $E(R_A) = IR \times \sigma_A$

"Full" fundamental law of active management:

$$E(R_A) = (TC)(IC)\sqrt{BR}\sigma_A$$

Sharpe-ratio-maximizing aggressiveness level:

$$STD(R_A) = \frac{IR}{SR_B}STD(R_B)$$

Execution Algorithms: Break an order down into smaller pieces to minimize market impact.
High-Frequency Algorithms: Programs that trade on real-time market data to pursue profits.

ISBN: 978-1-4754-5984-5

9 781475 459845

EQUITY continued...

- FCF is related to profitability.
- Controlling shareholder perspective.

Use residual income (RI) when:
- Firm lacks dividend history.
- Expected FCF is negative.

Gordon Growth Model (GGM)
Assumes perpetual dividend growth rate:

$$V_0 = \frac{D_1}{r - g}$$

Most appropriate for mature, stable firms. Limitations are:
- Very sensitive to estimates of r and g.
- Difficult with non-dividend stocks.
- Difficult with unpredictable growth patterns (use multi-stage model).

Present Value of Growth Opportunities

$$V_0 = \frac{E_1}{r} + PVGO$$

2-Stage Growth Model
Step 1: Calculate high-growth period dividends.
Step 2: Use GGM for terminal value at end of high-growth period.
Step 3: Discount interim dividends and terminal value to time zero to find stock value.

H-Model

$$V_0 = \frac{\left[D_0 \times (1 + g_L)\right]}{r - g_L} + \frac{\left[D_0 \times H \times (g_S - g_L)\right]}{r - g_L}$$

Sustainable Growth Rate: $b \times ROE$.

Solving for Required Return
For Gordon (or stable growth) model:

$$r = \frac{D_1}{P_0} + g$$

Free Cash Flow to Firm (FCFF)
Assuming depreciation is the only NCC:
- FCFF = NI + Dep + [Int × (1 – tax rate)] – FCInv – WCInv.
- FCFF = [EBIT × (1 – tax rate)] + Dep – FCInv – WCInv.
- FCFF = [EBITDA × (1 – tax rate)] + (Dep × tax rate) – FCInv – WCInv.
- FCFF = CFO + [Int × (1 – tax rate)] – FCInv.

Free Cash Flow to Equity (FCFE)
- FCFE = FCFF – [Int × (1 – tax rate)] + Net borrowing.
- FCFE = NI + Dep – FCInv – WCInv + Net borrowing.
- FCFE = NI – [(1 – DR) × (FCInv – Dep)] – [(1 – DR) × WCInv]. (*Used to forecast.*)

Single-Stage FCFF/FCFE Models
- For FCFF valuation: $V_0 = \dfrac{FCFF_1}{WACC - g}$
- For FCFE valuation: $V_0 = \dfrac{FCFE_1}{r - g}$

2-Stage FCFF/FCFE Models
Step 1: Calculate FCF in high-growth period.
Step 2: Use single-stage FCF model for terminal value at end of high-growth period.
Step 3: Discount interim FCF and terminal value to time zero to find stock value; use WACC for FCFF, r for FCFE.

Price to Earnings (P/E) Ratio
Problems with P/E:
- If earnings < 0, P/E meaningless.
- Volatile, transitory portion of earnings makes interpretation difficult.
- Management discretion over accounting choices affects reported earnings.

Justified P/E

leading P/E $= \dfrac{1 - b}{r - g}$

trailing P/E $= \dfrac{(1 - b)(1 + g)}{r - g}$

Justified dividend yield:

$$\frac{D_0}{P_0} = \frac{r - g}{1 + g}$$

Normalization Methods
- Historical average EPS.
- Average ROE.

Price to Book (P/B) Ratio
Advantages:
- BV almost always > 0.
- BV more stable than EPS.
- Measures NAV of financial institutions.

Disadvantages:
- Size differences cause misleading comparisons.
- Influenced by accounting choices.
- BV ≠ MV due to inflation/technology.

$$\text{justified } P/B = \frac{ROE - g}{r - g}$$

Price to Sales (P/S) Ratio
Advantages:
- Meaningful even for distressed firms.
- Sales revenue not easily manipulated.
- Not as volatile as P/E ratios.
- Useful for mature, cyclical, and start-up firms.

Disadvantages:
- High sales ≠ imply high profits and cash flows.
- Does not capture cost structure differences.
- Revenue recognition practices still distort sales.

$$\text{justified } P/S = \frac{PM_0 \times (1 - b)(1 + g)}{r - g}$$

DuPont Model

$$ROE = \left[\frac{\text{net income}}{\text{sales}}\right] \times \left[\frac{\text{sales}}{\text{total assets}}\right] \times \left[\frac{\text{total assets}}{\text{equity}}\right]$$

Price to Cash Flow Ratios
Advantages:
- Cash flow harder to manipulate than EPS.
- More stable than P/E.
- Mitigates earnings quality concerns.

Disadvantages:
- Difficult to estimate true CFO.
- FCFE better but more volatile.

Method of Comparables
- Firm multiple > benchmark implies overvalued.
- Firm multiple < benchmark implies undervalued.
- Fundamentals that affect multiple should be similar between firm and benchmark.

Residual Income Models
- RI = $E_t - (r \times B_{t-1})$ = (ROE – r) × B_{t-1}
- Single-stage RI model:

$$V_0 = B_0 + \left[\frac{(ROE - r) \times B_0}{r - g}\right]$$

- Multistage RI valuation: $V_0 = B_0$ + (PV of interim high-growth RI) + (PV of continuing RI)

Economic Value Added®
- EVA = NOPAT – $WACC; NOPAT = EBIT(1 – t).

Private Equity Valuation

$$DLOC = 1 - \left[\frac{1}{1 + \text{Control Premium}}\right]$$

Total discount = 1 – [(1 – DLOC)(1 – DLOM)]. The DLOM varies with the following.
- An impending IPO or firm sale ↓ DLOM.
- The payment of dividends ↓ DLOM.
- Earlier, higher payments ↓ DLOM.
- Restrictions on selling stock ↑ DLOM.
- A greater pool of buyers ↓ DLOM.
- Greater risk and value uncertainty ↑ DLOM.

FIXED INCOME

Price of a T-period zero-coupon bond:

$$P_T = \frac{1}{\left(1 + S_T\right)^T}$$

Forward price of zero-coupon bond:

$$F_{(j,k)} = \frac{1}{\left[1 + f(j,k)\right]^k}$$

Forward pricing model:

$$F_{(j,k)} = \frac{P_{(j+k)}}{P_j}$$

Forward rate model:

$$[1 + f(j,k)]^k = [1 + S_{(j+k)}]^{(j+k)} / (1 + S_j)^j$$

"Riding the yield curve": Holding bonds with maturity > investment horizon, with upward sloping yield curve.

swap spread$_t$ = swap rate$_t$ – treasury yield$_t$

TED spread:
= (3-month LIBOR rate) – (3-month T-bill rate)

Libor-OIS spread
= LIBOR rate – "overnight indexed swap" rate

Term Structure of Interest Rates
Traditional theories:
- Unbiased (pure) expectations theory.
- Local expectations theory.
- Liquidity preference theory.
- Segmented markets theory.
- Preferred habitat theory.

Modern term structure models:
- Cox-Ingersoll-Ross: $dr = a(b-r)dt + \sigma\sqrt{r}dz$
- Vasicek model: $dr = a(b - r)dt + \sigma dz$
- Ho-Lee model: $dr_t = \theta_t dt + \sigma dz_t$

Managing yield curve shape risk:
$$\Delta P/P \approx -D_L \Delta x_L - D_S \Delta x_S - D_C \Delta x_C$$
(L = *level*, S = *steepness*, C = *curvature*)

Yield volatility: *Long-term* ← uncertainty regarding the real economy and inflation.
Short term ← uncertainty re: monetary policy.
Long-term yield volatility is generally lower than volatility in short-term yields.

Value of option embedded in a bond:
$$V_{call} = V_{straight\ bond} - V_{callable\ bond}$$
$$V_{put} = V_{putable\ bond} - V_{straight\ bond}$$

When interest rate volatility increases:
$$V_{call\ option} \uparrow, V_{put\ option} \uparrow, V_{callable\ bond} \downarrow, V_{putable\ bond} \uparrow$$

Upward sloping yield curve: Results in lower call value and higher put value.

When binomial tree assumed volatility *increases*:
- computed OAS of a *callable* bond *decreases*.
- computed OAS of a *putable* bond *increases*.

$$\text{effective duration} = \frac{BV_{-\Delta y} - BV_{+\Delta y}}{2 \times BV_0 \times \Delta y}$$

$$\text{effective convexity} = \frac{BV_{-\Delta y} + BV_{+\Delta y} - (2 \times BV_0)}{BV_0 \times \Delta y^2}$$

Effective duration:
- ED (callable bond) ≤ ED (straight bond).
- ED (putable bond) ≤ ED (straight bond).
- ED (zero-coupon) ≈ maturity of the bond.
- ED fixed-rate bond < maturity of the bond.
- ED of floater ≈ time (years) to next reset.

continued on next page...

One-sided durations: Callables have lower down-duration; putables have lower up-duration.

Value of a capped floater
= straight floater value − embedded cap value

Value of a floored floater
= straight floater value + embedded floor value

Minimum value of convertible bond
= *greater of* conversion value or straight value

Conversion value of convertible bond
= market price of stock × conversion ratio

Market conversion price

$$= \frac{\text{market price of convertible bond}}{\text{conversion ratio}}$$

Market conversion premium per share
= market conversion price − stock's market price

Market conversion premium ratio

$$= \frac{\text{market conversion premium per share}}{\text{market price of common stock}}$$

Premium over straight value

$$= \left(\frac{\text{market price of convertible bond}}{\text{straight value}} \right) - 1$$

Callable and putable convertible bond value
= straight value of bond
+ value of call option on stock
− value of call option on bond
+ value of put option on bond

recovery rate = % money *received* upon default

Loss given default (%) = 100 − recovery rate

Expected loss = prob. of default × loss given default

Present value of expected loss
= (risky bond value) − (risk-free bond value)

Structural model of corporate credit risk:
• value of risky debt = value of risk-free debt − value of put option on the company's assets
• equity ≈ European call on company assets

Reduced form models: Impose assumptions on the output of a structural model.

Credit analysis of ABS:
• ABS do not default but lose value w/defaults.
• Modeled w/probability of loss, loss given default, expected loss, present value of the loss.

Credit Default Swap (CDS): Upon credit event, protection buyer compensated by protection seller.

Index CDS: Multiple borrowers, equally weighted.

Default: Occurrence of a credit event.

Common credit events in CDS agreements: Bankruptcy, failure to pay, restructuring.

CDS spread: Higher for a *higher* probability of default and for a *higher* loss given default.

Hazard rate = conditional probability of default.
expected loss$_t$ = (hazard rate)$_t$ × (loss given default)$_t$

Upfront CDS payment (paid by protection buyer)
= PV(protection leg) − PV(premium leg)
≈ (CDS spread − CDS coupon) × duration × NP

Change in value for a CDS after inception
≈ chg in spread × duration × notional principal

DERIVATIVES

Forward contract price (cost-of-carry model)

$$FP = S_0 \times (1 + R_f)^T \qquad S_0 = \frac{FP}{(1 + R_f)^T}$$

Price of equity forward with discrete dividends
FP(on an equity security) = $(S_0 - PVD) \times (1 + R_f)^T$

Value of forward on dividend-paying stock

$$V_t(\text{long position}) = [S_t - PVD_t] - \left[\frac{FP}{(1 + R_f)^{(T-t)}} \right]$$

Forward on equity index with continuous dividends

$$FP(\text{on an equity index}) = S_0 \times e^{\left(R_f^c - \delta^c \right) \times T}$$
$$= \left(S_0 \times e^{-\delta^c \times T} \right) \times e^{R_f^c \times T}$$

where:
R_f^c = *continuously compounded risk-free rate*
δ^c = *continuously compounded dividend yield*

Forward price on a coupon-paying bond:

$$FP(\text{on a fixed income security})$$
$$= (S_0 - PVC) \times (1 + R_f)^T$$
or
$$= S_0 \times (1 + R_f)^T - FVC$$

Value of a forward on a coupon-paying bond:

$$V_t(\text{long}) = [S_t - PVC_t] - \left[\frac{FP}{(1 + R_f)^{(T-t)}} \right]$$

Price of a bond futures contract:
FP = [(full price)$(1+R_f)^T - AI_T - FVC$]
full price = quoted spot price + AI_0

Quoted bond futures price:

$$QFP = \text{forward price / conversion factor}$$
$$= \left[(\text{full price})(1+R_f)^T - AI_T - FVC \right] \left(\frac{1}{CF} \right)$$

Price of a currency forward contract:

$$F_T = S_0 \times \frac{(1 + R_{PC})^T}{(1 + R_{BC})^T}$$

Value of a currency forward contract

$$V_t = \frac{[FP_t - FP] \times (\text{contract size})}{(1 + r_{PC})^{(T-t)}}$$

Currency forward price (continuous time):

$$F_T = S_0 \times e^{\left(R_{PC}^c - R_{BC}^c \right) \times T}$$

Swap fixed rate:

$$C = \frac{1 - Z_4}{Z_1 + Z_2 + Z_3 + Z_4}$$

where: $Z_n = 1/(1+R_n)$ = price of n-period zero-coupon bond per $ of principal

Value of interest rate swap to fixed payer:

$$= \sum Z \times (SFR_{New} - SFR_{Old}) \times \frac{\text{days}}{360} \times \text{notional}$$

Binomial stock tree probabilities:

$$\pi_U = \text{probability of up move} = \frac{1 + R_f - D}{U - D}$$

$$\pi_D = \text{probability of a down move} = (1 - \pi_U)$$

Put-call parity:
$$S_0 + P_0 = C_0 + PV(X)$$

Put-call parity when the stock pays dividends:
$$P_0 + S_0 e^{-\delta T} = C_0 + e^{-rT}X$$

Dynamic delta hedging

$$\text{# of short call options} = \frac{\text{# shares hedged}}{\text{delta of call option}}$$

$$\text{# of long put options} = -\frac{\text{# shares hedged}}{\text{delta of put option}}$$

Change in option value
$\Delta C \approx$ call delta × ΔS + ½ gamma × ΔS^2
$\Delta P \approx$ put delta × ΔS + ½ gamma × ΔS^2

Option value using arbitrage-free pricing portfolio

$$C_0 = hS_0 + \frac{(-hS^+ + C^+)}{(1 + R_f)} = hS_0 + \frac{(-hS^- + C^-)}{(1 + R_f)}$$

$$P_0 = hS_0 + \frac{(-hS^- + P^-)}{(1 + R_f)} = hS_0 + \frac{(-hS^+ + P^+)}{(1 + R_f)}$$

Black–Scholes–Merton option valuation model

$$C_0 = S_0 e^{-\delta T} N(d_1) - e^{-rT} X N(d_2)$$
$$P_0 = e^{-rT} X N(-d_2) - S_0 e^{-\delta T} N(-d_1)$$

where:

δ = continuously compounded dividend yield

$$d_1 = \frac{\ln(S/X) + (r - \delta + \sigma^2/2)T}{\sigma\sqrt{T}}$$

$$d_2 = d_1 - \sigma\sqrt{T}$$

$S_0 e^{-\delta T}$ = stock price, less PV of dividends

OPTION STRATEGIES:

Covered call = long stock + short call

Protective put = long stock + long put

Bull spread: Long option with low exercise price + short option with higher exercise price. Profit if underlying $↑.

Bear spread: exercise price of long > exc. price of short

Collar = covered call + protective put

Long straddle = long call + long put (*with same strike*). Pays off if future volatility is higher.

Calendar spread: Sell one option + buy another at a maturity where higher volatility is expected.

Long calendar spread: Short near-dated call + long long-dated call. (*Short calendar spread is opposite.*)

Breakeven volatility analysis

$$\sigma_{annual} = \%\Delta P \times \sqrt{\frac{252}{\text{trading days until maturity}}}$$

where

$$\%\Delta P = \frac{\text{absolute(breakeven price} - \text{current price)}}{\text{current price}}$$

ALTERNATIVE INVESTMENTS

Value of property using direct capitalization:
rental income if fully occupied
+ other income
= potential gross income
− vacancy and collection loss
= effective gross income
− operating expense
= net operating income

$$\text{cap rate} = \frac{NOI_1}{\text{comparable sales price}}$$

$$\text{value} = V_0 = \frac{NOI_1}{\text{cap rate}} \text{ or } V_0 = \frac{\text{stabilized NOI}}{\text{cap rate}}$$

Property value based on "All Risks Yield":
value = V_0 = rent$_1$ / ARY

Value of a property using gross income multiplier:

$$\text{gross income multiplier} = \frac{\text{sales price}}{\text{gross income}}$$

Term and reversion property valuation approach:
total property value
= PV of term rent + PV reversion to ERV

Layer approach:
total property value
= PV of term rent + PV of incremental rent

continued on next page...